Biography®

Queen
CLEOPATRA

Tom Streissguth

A&E®

Lerner Publications Company
Minneapolis

Copyright © 2000 by Lerner Publications Company.

Lerner Publications Company
A Division of Lerner Publishing Group
241 First Avenue North
Minneapolis, Minnesota 55401 U.S.A.

Website address: www.lernerbooks.com

Library of Congress Cataloging-in-Publication Data

Streissguth, Thomas, 1958-
    Queen Cleopatra / Tom Streissguth.
    Includes bibliographical references and index.
    Summary: Presents the life of the Egyptian queen who lived from 69 B.C.E. to 30 B.C.E.
    ISBN 0-8225-4946-8 (alk. paper)
    1. Cleopatra, Queen of Egypt, d. 30 B.C.—Juvenile literature.
2. Queens—Egypt—Biography—Juvenile literature. [1. Cleopatra, Queen of Egypt, d. 30 B.C. 2. Kings, queens, rulers, etc.] I. Title. II. Series
DT92.7.S88 2000
932'.021'92—dc21
    [B]   98-49250

Manufactured in the United States of America
1 2 3 4 5 6 – JR – 05 04 03 02 01 00

CONTENTS

Cleopatra arrives in Tarsus, a city in Asia Minor, to meet the Roman general Mark Antony.

Chapter **ONE**

AN ANCIENT LAND RULED BY STRANGERS

ON A SPRING DAY IN THE YEAR **41** B.C., PEOPLE of the city of Tarsus in Asia Minor (part of what has since become Turkey) gathered along the banks of the Cydnus River. An immense barge, its long oars slowly dipping into the water, was sailing up the river and directly toward them. The spectators were about to witness a spectacle that none of them would ever forget: Cleopatra, queen of Egypt, was arriving to greet the most powerful leader of the Roman world. A famous Greek historian named Plutarch later wrote:

> She came sailing up the river Cydnus in a barge with gilded stern and outspread sails of purple, while oars of silver beat time to the music of flutes and fifes and harps. . . . Her maids were

dressed like sea nymphs and graces, some steering at the rudder, some working at the ropes.

The fleet and royal flagship of this wealthy queen, Cleopatra VII of Egypt, anchored at the river's edge. Cleopatra had been summoned here by the Roman general Marcus Antonius, or Mark Antony. While Cleopatra ruled only Egypt, Antony held sway over Tarsus and hundreds of other Roman territories in Asia Minor and the eastern Mediterranean region. But Mark Antony's power and titles did not intimidate the haughty, majestic Cleopatra. In a display of pride and independence, she summoned the Roman general to come down to the river's edge to meet *her*. As more people rushed out of the town and down to the riverbank, Antony found himself alone with a few of his guards, waiting in vain for the queen.

Antony was a proud but good-natured man. Having important matters to settle with this queen, he humbly marched to her royal ship, greeted her servants, and climbed aboard like an ordinary guest. There, he and Cleopatra struck a bargain that would change their lives and the history of the Western world.

THE ANCIENT LAND OF EGYPT

Cleopatra's Egypt lay along the banks of the Nile River in northern Africa. The waters of the Nile flowed northward through a fertile valley, which supplied the grain, fruit, dates, papyrus, and other valuable goods that made the country wealthy. For thousands of years, Egyptian pharaohs (monarchs) had ruled here. They lived in great palaces, and were deified, or worshipped as gods, by their people.

The ancient Egyptians were polytheistic: they worshiped many different gods. Re, for example, was the sun god, while Horus was the god of heaven. Osiris was the god of the dead and the underworld. Set was his brother, an evil god. Isis was the sister of Osiris and was worshiped as the protector of the dead and as the divine mother. At one time, Amon was the most important god in the Egyptian pantheon. In the city of Thebes, once the royal capital, an immense temple was dedicated to Amon. Eventually, the Egyptians combined the deities Amon and Re, creating Amon-Re. Known as the most powerful of all the gods, Amon-Re was symbolized by a living bull that inhabited a temple of its own at Thebes.

In 332 B.C., Alexander the Great, a young leader from Macedonia (a kingdom in northern Greece), marched his army south through Asia Minor, Syria, and Palestine, and conquered Egypt. Fascinated by the Egyptian religion, Alexander made a pilgrimage, or holy journey, to the oasis of Siwah in Egypt's western desert. In Siwah, a temple dedicated to the god Amon-Re stood atop a rocky hill. Alexander made his offering to Amon-Re and was in turn recognized by the priests of Siwah as the son and incarnation (rebirth) of the god.

After his pilgrimage to Siwah, Alexander conquered huge areas in the Middle East, Central Asia, and the valley of the Indus River in India. But in 323 B.C., he suddenly died of a fever in the city of Babylon (an ancient capital in what is now Iraq). His generals Antigonus, Seleucis, and Ptolemy, who had fought by his side for many years, then divided his most powerful states among themselves. Antigonus chose to rule over Macedonia, Seleucis chose Syria and Persia (modern-day Iran), and Ptolemy decided on Egypt.

Ptolemy had Alexander's body brought to Alexandria, the city Alexander had founded in 332 B.C. along Egypt's Mediterranean coast. Alexandria lay on a narrow isthmus between the Mediterranean Sea and Lake Mareotis, just west of the Nile River's delta. Although the city was still small, it was attracting many settlers from Greece, Macedonia, and other parts of Alexander's empire.

Ptolemy laid Alexander's body to rest in an elaborate tomb called the Sema. In the eyes of the Egyptians, this act, and the presence of Alexander's body in their homeland, gave Ptolemy a strong claim as the successor to Alexander. To further convince the Egyptians that he was worthy of ruling over them, Ptolemy claimed he was descended from the god Amon-Re. In the year 305 B.C., Ptolemy proclaimed himself Ptolemy I, successor of the ancient pharaohs and the divine ruler of Egypt. The Ptolemaic dynasty, or reign, had begun.

Cleopatra's Mediterranean
World, 51 B.C.

■ Roman Provinces

RED SEA

EGYPTIAN KINGDOM

Nile R.

Alexandria

Pelusium

JUDAEA

ARABIA

SYRIA

PARTHIAN EMPIRE

Euphrates R.

Tigris R.

ARMENIA

Antioch

CYPRUS

CILICIA

Tarsus

Cydnus R.

BITHYNIA-PONTUS

ASIA MINOR

Ephesus

BLACK SEA

MEDITERRANEAN SEA

CYRENE

MACEDONIA

Actium

ARCHAEA (GREECE)

ILLYRICUM

Brundisium

Tarentum

ITALY

Rome

AFRICA

SARDINIA

SICILY

CORSICA

NUMIDIA

CISALPINE GAUL

TRANSALPINE GAUL

GAUL

NEARER SPAIN

THE PTOLEMAIC RULERS

As an outsider, Ptolemy knew he must adopt the signs and symbols of the pharaohs in order to win the Egyptian people's support. He held ceremonies in which he was worshiped by the people, and directed artisans to depict him as a god in temple carvings and inscriptions.

Like Alexander before him, Ptolemy wanted to build Alexandria into a great city. A Greek architect, Deinocrates, had planned Alexandria's streets and designed its buildings. Alexandria had a long, wide main street known as the Canopus and two large harbors, separated by a mole (a narrow breakwater built of stone and earth). The city steadily grew into a center of trade between Europe, Arabia, and India. Egypt's merchants sold grain as well as ivory, gold, and valuable ostrich eggs from other parts of Africa. Alexandria's textiles, glass, jewelry, pottery, and metal goods displayed the finest workmanship in the Mediterranean world. In Ptolemy's time, Alexandria was already on its way to becoming the busiest and wealthiest port city in the entire Mediterranean region.

Ptolemy also worked to bring the advanced Greek culture and science to Egypt. To attain his goal, Ptolemy built the Museum, a school where Greek teachers educated and trained the children of wealthy Alexandrians. He also commissioned the Library, a part of the Museum where Alexandrian scholars collected the works of well-known Greek playwrights, poets, philosophers, mathematicians, astronomers, and doctors. This collection of hundreds of thousands of papyrus scrolls served as a vast storehouse of the ancient world's knowledge and literature and would become the foundation of science and culture for the Western world.

For all its wealth, Alexandria remained an isolated city. Many Alexandrians were settlers from Greece and other regions who knew very little of Egypt outside their own city. Instead, they traveled and traded in the lands along the Mediterranean Sea, where the language of trade was Greek. (Ptolemy and most of his successors never even bothered to learn the Egyptian language.) To these settlers, the land to the south, beyond Lake Mareotis, was a different and sometimes dangerous world. Here other settlers amassed huge estates and treated the peasants who worked the land as slaves. As they had for centuries, native-born Egyptians were forced to work on the canals and dikes that were designed to make the land more productive for wealthy landowners.

In the Nile Valley, life under Ptolemy went on much as it had for thousands of years. Poor peasants lived in small villages, farmed the land, and traveled the Nile in boats made of wooden planks or reeds. They carefully watched the annual flood of the Nile, which began in the late spring and continued for several months. In good years, the Nile generously watered fields and crops, bringing abundance; in poor years, it

THE HELLENISTIC WORLD

The fourth century B.C. was a turbulent time in Greece. Ancient Greeks lived in dozens of independent city-states bound together by a common language, religion, and culture, and were constantly at war with one another. In 338 B.C., eighteen-year-old Macedonian prince Alexander helped his father, Phillip II, conquer the Greek city-states. Alexander then went on to conquer vast lands in Africa, the Middle East, and India under his own leadership.

As a boy, Alexander had been tutored by the Greek philosopher Aristotle. Aristotle, considered one of the most influential thinkers in Western culture, taught that the ability to reason set people apart from animals. He believed that the ability to achieve balance and harmony in life through philosophy, science, and the arts set civilized cultures apart from barbaric societies.

As conqueror, Alexander the Great, as he was known, sought to spread Hellenic (Greek) customs and religion to the people of his new territories. His death in 323 B.C. marked the beginning of what historians call the Hellenistic period. In Hellenistic times, Alexander's generals established new dynasties and settled in nations Alexander had conquered. Along with the generals came settlers from Greece and other territories. Greek became the international language of the times, and philosophies based on the ideas of Aristotle and other leading thinkers were widely discussed and followed. Many of the Hellenistic thinkers lived in Egypt, where they studied and taught at an Alexandrian school called the Museum.

There were three primary groups of Hellenistic philosophers. They were mainly interested in how people could achieve a peaceful state of mind. Cynics believed that people should strive for virtue over all else. Epicureans were dedicated to pleasing the senses and achieving happiness by avoiding pain. Stoics thought that happiness resulted when people accepted life—both the good and the bad—as it came.